The Orchards of Syon

Books by Geoffrey Hill

POETRY

For the Unfallen

King Log

Mercian Hymns

Tenebræ

The Mystery of the Charity of Charles Péguy

New and Collected Poems, 1952–1992

Canaan

The Triumph of Love

Speech! Speech!

The Orchards of Syon

PROSE

The Lords of Limit:
Essays on Literature and Ideas

The Enemy's Country:
Words, Contexture, and Other Circumstances of Language

POETIC DRAMA

Henrik Ibsen's 'Brand':
A Version for the Stage

THE
ORCHARDS
OF SYON

Geoffrey Hill

COUNTERPOINT

Washington, D.C.

Library of Congress Cataloging-in-Publication Data

Hill, Geoffrey.
The Orchards of Syon / Geoffrey Hill.
p. cm.
ISBN 1-58243-166-3 (alk. paper)
1. Christian poetry, English.   1. Title.
PR6015.I4735 O73 2002
821'.914–dc21   2001047245

Printed in the United States of America
on acid-free paper that meets the American National Standards
Institute Z39 – 48 Standard ∞

COUNTERPOINT
P.O. Box 65793
Washington, D.C. 20035-5793

Counterpoint is a member of the Perseus Books Group

FIRST EDITION

To my children and grandchildren

Later, but before I had become a student of theology, that truth of which I have spoken struck me like a radiant light of grace. It seemed that I saw, though at a distance, within the image or form of Truth (this being wholly transparent), God's grace already present in time as in nature, before any good works existed.

—THOMAS BRADWARDINE, *De Causa Dei*

Tom Brangwen's mood of inspiration began to pass away. He forgot all about it, and was soon roaring and shouting with the rest...Only the bride and bridegroom sat with shining eyes and strange, bright faces, and scarcely sang, or only with just moving lips.

. . .

The five men went out. The night was flashing with stars. Sirius blazed like a signal at the side of the hill. Orion, stately and magnificent, was sloping along...

'It's a fine night,' said Tom.

—D. H. LAWRENCE, *The Rainbow*

Everything was at rest, free, and immortal.

—THOMAS TRAHERNE, *Centuries of Meditations*

The Orchards of Syon

I

Now there is no due season. Do not
mourn unduly. You have sometimes said
that I project a show more
stressful than delightful. Watch my hands
confabulate their shadowed rhetoric,
gestures of benediction; maledictions
by arrangement. For us there is
no deadline, neither for stand nor standoff.
I can prolong the act at times
to rival Augustine, this shutter
play among words, befitting
a pact with light, the contra-Faustian heist
from judgement to mercy.
I shall promote our going and coming,
as shadows, in expressive light; take
my belief, if only through a process
taxing salvation — may I proceed? —
not merely to divert with faith and fiction,
to ease peregrination, what a life!
Has it ever been staged
seriously outside Spain, I mean
La vida es sueño? Tell me, is this the way
to the Orchards of Syon
where I left you thinking I would return?

Something escapes committal; in my name
recalls itself to being. Mystic
durables are not the prime good, nor
lust the sole licenser. Shakespeare
clearly heard many voices. No secret:
voicing means hearing, at a price a gift,
affliction chiefly, whereas despair
clamps and is speechless. Donne in his time
also heard voices he preserved on wax
cylinders. Some of these I possess
and am possessed by. Persistence tells,
even when you are past speech, gurneyed
from *Death's Duel*. As for posterity,
whose lips are sealed, I do prefer
Polish to Czech ^l though, not speaking
either language, I am unable to say
why. Starting with these,
I wish I understood myself
more clearly or less well.
Go back to cast off several lives. Find
all have godlike elements
divided among them: such suffering,
you can imagine, driven, murderous,
albeit under notice of grace.

La vida es sueño as shadow-play. This
takes me back. Genuflect to the gutted
tabernacle, no-one will wonder in what sense
words are consequential to the cartoon.
How is this life adjudged
derelict, a stress-bearer since Eden?
Think ahead: your name
finally out of alignment, its
dates crammed in; they might be self-inflicted
wounds of morose delectation
borne lightly out of primal throes, a last
remittance from doomed childhood.
Unwise or wise choices do make
gymnasts of anchorites, if that
means what Í mean. You say you have me there
which is all we have here, in the Orchards
of Syon that are like Goldengrove
season beyond season. Neither day nor hour
to determine the tinder
chemistry of exchange. If I were you, would
you believe? Ripe vastage of estate,
the Fall revived with death-songs. Set this down
as anomy's coherence, and the full-
blooded scrub maples torch themselves in the swamp.

We are — what, all of us? — near death. So wave
me your solution. *Cupio dissolvi*,
Saul's vital near-death experience more
sandblasted than lasered. *Beam
us up, Asrael*. High talk, dissolution
expansive, all pervasive; here it coils
back into density: dark angel, fused,
rubberoid, shrunk, foetal, as though raked
from Zeppelin ashes. Immortal
Death, lovely suppliant!
Orphée I saw six times in the one week.
Du calme counsels the Princess, Maria
Casarès, newly *enceinte* with sorrow
not hers alone. Her tragic shadow — pulled
through — down and across — is swept
off the blank end wall. Truth not so hot,
unobliging, even at the last count.
I understand Hell's surreal ruins to be
those of the blitzed Académie de St Cyr,
with wind machines off camera, all elements
miming a solemn music.
Bite on yr death wish. As for faith,
expose it finally, like ignorance.
Coming or going, do the circuits again.

V

Baroque says nothing broken, though to break
off labours the point,
and it judders and all.
Nonetheless I would clinch this
as music's invocation, the tuned
drums *glissando*. You
can elide changes of pressure. I believe
creation ís self-healing, a self-stanched
issue of blood. It is also
furtherance of slow exile, but enjoy —
best to enjoy — riding that *vague*.
Requite self-envying, to eat the heart out
for the heart's satisfaction, is this
wisdom? Well, as the wise man said,
I know it when I see it. So much
of time is rubble. Under the sky's
great clearances, not oúr time only.
How beautiful the world unrecognized
through most of seventy years, the may-tree filling
with visionary silent laughter. *Comme si
l'aubépine* — FRÉNAUD — *était un présage.*
The hawthorn all the more fulfilling its beauty.
Comme si les dieux nous avaient aimés.
As if the gods even now had faith in us.

I know breakthrough as I tell
the dream surpassed. *The Art of Fugue* resembles
water-springs in the Negev. No
longer much to write home about,
endurances give us forty years
post-visionary so far. Weak fulfilment
while the joke empties. This is a joke?
Not when ajar. *Adieu, mon capitaine*,
go spare, go Immelmann, spared flamer,
straight through the climacteric, no avoidance.
In threads of chaos anarchy remains
the cryptic absolute whose clue is reason,
lost achievements, music lost among them,
deeper than we imagined, protracted
jealous exhaustion holding the floor.
Applaud, won't you, if only first time round,
and I alone escaped to tell thee. Don't
abreact to all blind self-exposure
permitted the Resistance. Heavenly music!
As order moves by instinct I say trust
faith so far as it goes, or as far as you
can hold its attention. Cite EMMANUEL:
the man of sorrows whose blood burns us.
Le misericordieux qui nous brûle le sang.

Our fealties taken to be your places
of refuge and defence. Author? Author
is all one word, like Faculties. Can you
receive me? Unwise to make wise choices
too early. Incorrigible in any case
the human spirit or its spin-offs,
cogent, unreadable, and at some
personal cost a public nuisance:
not ineradicable but not soon
put down or uprooted. Best early flowering
or in the sere. Music arguably
not implicated in the loss of Eden,
held to its resolution. No
question an affirmation. Tell him he ís
alive — someone — and responsible. He may
respond to that, as to other electrodes,
as Lear to the sour-sweet music of viols,
as some to oils of unction or to Gospel.
Tune him to GOSPEL: *Over my head
I hear music, music in the air.* That
Gospel? Súre that Gospel! Thát sure
Gospel music in my head. Oh, my sole
sister, you, little sister-my-soul,
this mý Gospel, thís sure músic in mý head.

No mystery I tell you, though in the first
instance it ís a gift, one that you owe me,
the square-stemmed woundwort I have been brought
to consider, precious as peppercorn
once was. No description
merely for beauty's sake, so Flaubert said,
or wounded Maupassant, or someone poisonous.
You owe me, Albion, I should have added
in Ivor's name not mine. Let them be:
tenacity of accent, leaching phosphates,
stringy Welsh poppy, its alien yellow. Is it
anything of significance that I
ceased to attend? Headlands are where ploughs turned
back over Batty's durance. As I recall.
The labours of the months are now memory,
indigent wordplay, stubborn, isolate
language of inner exile.
The curlew's pitch distracts us from her nest.
But: end this for all in some shape other
than vexed bafflement; each triangular
wall-cope cladded with tight moss
springy as a terrier's pelt, buttonhole
emerald polypodae, sprung tremblers
within the burring air of the fell?

The year rounds, takes fragments round with it. Some
tryst this is, image-conscious iconoclast!
The well-worn pattern, familiar abutments,
abraded angles, in the nature of limestone,
unfinished to perfection. Say something, you
have a name for it. Curlews on call,
high and abroad, to be identified
quartering the topmost fields; and other
alarm cries, known but not placed, *chich
chich, chich chich*. Penumbrate, a lily
distinctly shines, talisman
to that which is key-cold ín me, and sealed.
Could be haemony, from some remote
and gracious fable, upholding the rod
or stem of sharp judgement, finally spared.
Are you still with us, spirit of difficult
forgiveness íf I may so term you? The man
is old; it is more than age he girns for.
And Í said: is there anything you think
you should tell me? Was there a mirror
and did it breathe cold speculation?
He is knackered and there are no
schemes to revive him. The year unlocks,
hunkers, swings, its anniversary-round.

Sleep to incubate diamond. What a find,
a self-awarded *donnée* if ever
I knew one. If that one was ever you,
wrestle, wrestle with me, my love, my dirty
fighter. I can't say much
plainer than that. *T'souviens-toi
Tom-mee?* Tom Wyatt, his lute and grating,
his torturing, tortured friends.
I place myself in a seven-year pre-
survival bracket, with options. Nod
if you can't speak and let me charge it
to my own account. The Lambeth
Prophecies, The Good Friday Agreement.
Even now I confess
difficulty in pronouncing ǀ súch wórds
as absolution. Suggested manual
of handsignals might work the trick.
Strophe after strophe. *Achilles*
from *Ajax*: power-loss imminent, the split
voice-tube welts blood. Dead Tragedy threatening,
death of Comedy is perhaps a worse
dereliction. Strophe after strophe
ever more catastrophic. Did I say
strophe? I meant salvo, sorry.

Begin with golden curtains; sometimes helps
to anticipate THE END. How did they make
insouciant comedy so like innocence?
By way of Ealing, charm in confusion
through to last checkpoints. Impudent,
feckless. Watch them frogmarched off.
The Day of Judgement (WATTS) dire codicil
to human mood and thought; elect
doctrine on show, its common other side
exposed in saturnalia. I salute
yr good self— the stout party — bounding
egalitarian cockiness its *forte*,
sensual, unfallen. Dreams have charted
levels of sleep both complex and perplexing
I understand. It's a safe bet we're all
potentially impotent. Again, you coúld
say that I give myself
to well-failed causes. If this failed
to make the last connection I'd be sorry
from my own viewpoint, rarely now entranced
by calf love, light-fingered cockneys. Pimlico
is not Silvertown ǀ though,
on the screen, it might appear so. Exit —
through heavy resistant side-doors — in a daze.

Might gain eras of promise, collages
of dashed peace, many-headed the field
rose, dog rose, tossing in bright squalls,
all things self-verifying. A ferrous
atmospheric tang between lightning-bouts
has similar potencies, its presentiments
in the instant abundance, superflux,
familiar chill inspiration, self-
charged shock beyond shock. Show how many
succeed, rising again undiscovered,
turning at a breath: exhalation,
threshold and lintel, the unknown
to be entered, yet to be desired;
on a timekeeper's schedule if need be.
Exhalation, ah, not inspiration! the Orchards
of Syon exhaling green into gold,
gold to candescent red. Like ancient
rhetoric, both florid and threadbare,
showing the *stemma*. Light-endowed
among the natural shades and shadows; heavy-
browed barbed rugosa, rain-hackled, a streaming
instant unreconciled, magnificently
thrown off— the coda,
the invoked finality ǀ the setting-out.

No: blessing not mercy. Not that I care
to chance it. Unless there glints our ransom.
Centuries of failed initiates exclaim
against these equities. Whatever
your name is, leaden Mercurius.
Let me review a sometime common
standing or vantage. Patchy weather, quick
showers gusting the fields like clouds of lime.
You thought us held by favours: see above.
Such are the starts of memory, abrupt
blessing slid from confusion. Await
new-fangled light, the slate roofs briefly
caught in scale-nets of silver, then
sheened with thin oils. These signals
I take as apprehension, new-aligned
poetry with truth, and Syon's Orchards
uncannily of the earth.
JEFFERIES' *ancient sunlight*, Williamson
perhaps turning more profit by the phrase.
But pass me over, angel. I've recast
my furthest revelation; it's as much
as you have witnessed, much as I have told:
a massive, shedding, insubstantial substance
blurred and refocused, blurred afresh by rain.

The fell, through brimming heat-haze, ashen grey,
in a few hours changes to graphite, coral,
rare Libyan sand colour or banded spectrum.
Distant flocks merge into limestone's half-light.
The full moon, now, rears with unhastening speed,
sketches the black ridge-end, slides thin lustre
downward aslant its gouged and watered scree.
Awe is not peace, not one of the sacred
duties in mediation. Memory
finds substance in itself. Whatever's brought,
one to the other, masking and unmasking,
by each particular shift of clarity
wrought and obscurely broken-in upon,
of serene witness, neither mine nor yours,
I will ask bristling centaury to translate.
Saved by immersion, sleep, forgetfulness,
the tinctured willow and frail-textured ash,
untrodden fern-sheaves, a raw-horned oak,
the wavering argents in the darkened river.
Later again, far higher on the fell,
a solitary lamp, *notturna lampa*,
night's focus focusing, LEOPARDI saw,
himself a stranger, once, returning late,
from some forsaken village festival.

Nothing untimely, since we are all
in time checked at dispersal, possibly
for keeps. *La vida es sueño?* I ought
to read it, before they say I haven't.
Memory proves forgetting. Take gipsylike
klezmer, soul music
not everywhere unheard, not at all times
accusingly silent. O Queen of Heaven,
now no wonder
description is trial being of the person
always on call, always answerable,
a witness that can barely be suppressed:
try loyalty or some such common oath.
But having to wake up and always
in a different place, always to the same
postlude of nightmare. *Crimen* is not
the root, *kómē* ís yr coiffure of fire,
martyrs who reap the flames. Presentable
tribute to the passing down of kings,
Poiesis a sufficient act, I almost
forgot to say this. Otherwise
the transient ever-repeated dream,
the all-forgetful. *La vida es sueño*
or something other. Other, that is, than death.

Cassandra at twenty, thanks to RONSARD. Or
reshape a clause from Petrarch's book, his thought
wedged in the solid nature of the world
like a doorstop or indeed a dossier.
Expatiate on this, or say *La vita
nuova* the limit. Or change views entirely.
Deep-rucked topsoil where brick lorries turn; Jim
Brindley's iron and stone; Boulton's coin-press;
Baskerville cutting, setting, his plain
and ornamental types; artificers'
resounding mastery of things hard laboured.
My masterwork this patched-up exhibition
and national treasure, memorial
of a non-event, our absurd love
put here to confront us — you can describe it
or I shall —
pace your half-provoking dismayed mirth.
Others such as we were and are themselves
still of sound mind.
Leave undefeated losers to make good.
Life's fatal dance moves as a simple
covenant with time, the circuits of our choice.
How would yoú stress PAVESE's axiom —
lavorare stanca — work till you drop?

Tri-towers, Christ-silos, rise from, retract
into, the broad Ouse levels. Roadside poppies,
hedged bindweed, still beautiful. The kempt fields
basking; intense the murmur of full summer,
more growl than murmur: coast-traffic snarled,
snarling. Hawks over the dual carriageways.
I've jolted from northward across the moors,
not entirely at peace. Memoranda for horizons
in travail — spirit-levels — steadiness
of outlook all too readily measured.
Broadly, I have the measure of myself,
mechanically at bay. I'd not resurrect
Goldengrove, other than as a grove in Syon:
sustainable anomaly, so I
can tell you, though too easily said.
Tommies' lore, re crucifixes and the like;
Tennyson's wild expenditure of bells;
suffering — Gurney's — his queer
politics; Owen transfixed by eros:
my difficulties are not with their
forever-earnest speech. The chorus
lines of road-rage shunt to yet more delay.
Masked somewhere, on one side or the other,
the time-struck Minster doles greed by the clock.

Comedic my control: with each new old
scenario, keep moving. In the Orchards
of Syon you can delve Los Angeles
or some other holy place.
Havergal Brian's Five Towns extorted
wealth from poverty, but with choral music
held as a birthright: well-tended ground
ripe for laying waste, the Great War.
Lawrence's Eastwood, Rosenberg
in Stepney and Whitechapel — I'm
ordered to speak plainly, let what ís
speak for itself, not to redeem the time
but to get even with it.
Glastonbury mislodged on its mud lake
with jackpot ignorance and freakish thorn;
York trafficking, gridlocking, organ-congas,
medieval hell-mouths less congested
than this sullen Minster. Anarchy coheres.
Incoherence coheres. Stupor animates.
Chaos ordains. But to what depth? Some demon
chobbles its rap-cassette, spits out
pathetic dreadlocks. I had forgotten
Donne's meta-theology. A road-drill
swallowed through tarred slab re-emerges fighting.

The Orchards of Syon

LUMEN OBSCURUM: Latin would be my guess.
Like *atemwende*. Take another walk
down to the river, where the darkening flood
churns beneath burnt-out alders, leaps and yaws
across — between — its millstone rocks, unwieldy.
Whatever's cryptic is Polish. Explain that.
Polish blood, capillaries of Hypnos,
or Romany, or Semitic. Make a wish,
if only in sign-language, and I'll find you,
Mateusz six, twenty-one, our chalk mark.
You could render
atemwende as breath-glitch. Speak in whispers.
Ostracizm's a small foothill town
in the Carpathians that retires at dusk,
battening rumours, telling its safe houses.
Tenacity itself can drive
only so far. WAT's posthumous *lumen*
obscurum holds fast; at the nub of things
settled, creaturely, its fabulous glim
invisible to most. So how did he know?
Through enigmatic channels, very clearly:
smoked them all out, grudge-heavy honey-bees
living off self-remitted spoil of the hive.
Where your treasure is, there is your heart also.

Consider these cauteries life-tokens
to a hapless though not hopeless intelligence.
Cicatrice is no dead insect. The balm-
bearing trees are incised. New skin
sets itself in patterns of the old wounds.
Denn wo euer Schatz ist, da ist auch
euer Hertz. Spirit's a tad elsewhere,
brown on the ceiling, caught among the drains,
stashed in some mezzanine. Where your treasure
lies, there your heart lies also. Is this even
to be thought? Whereas each moment's
epiphany's much like a betrayal
of held breath, I feel the need to swing
things and let go. Hourly, on the hour,
somebody fresh | floored by the virus
of inspiration. As for mischance, I know
halogen projects Chinese characters
deep into the closed
circus of my eyelids. I'm not blind,
nor blind the world's designer randomness:
schwarzrot of the dying rose, the thick
greenwarped Spanish glass; clashed consanguinity,
rioja against rioja; diverse
affinities; unassuaged; rejoicing.

Sensual intellectualism now the rage
no longer, dead Ingeborg, lost
surrogate in the lion's mouth, *nella
Bocca di Leone*. If we could
recommence this, what would I have to say?
The first one and a bit lines might hold,
perhaps, for a good kick- or jump-start,
like getting this short story off the ground.
I think I prefer you without makeup
as I suspect Celan did also.
I'm less sure of the plump Italian; he
loved young Jewish women — Irma Brandeis,
Dora Markus — but moved on, to Opera,
which could have brought you together. So where,
then, might we have met? Monteverdi's *La
bufera e altro? Il buffo e altro? The Storm
Flah-Flah* is where I would endeavour,
now, to transport you in imagination:
ad ulteriorem ripam, the refuelling
autumns of Goldengrove; all this despite
Dis's archaic hold, plus evidence
that you were mishandled by death's angel
yourself; or even that this *Cantilena*
is not a flying-boat.

Memory is its own vision, a gift of sight,
from which thought step aside, and frequently,
into the present, where we have possession
more and more denied us. I shall not
deny yoú without recollection.
Query: how far ascribe this to a failed,
no, failing, motor control. I am not less
careful or curious of our durance, *the eye's*
elaboration of tears, M^{RS} BEETON's
beautiful phrase. She failed at twenty-eight
and went unwept by me. Now you also,
sine nomine, if that is what you are,
earthy-etherial, I desire you
to fathom what I mean. What dó I mean?
I think you are a muse or something,
though too early rejected. The dank
Triassic marl, sandstone like mouldered plaster,
can't all-inhold you. From Burcot to Worms Ash
the rock sweats and trickles, even in winter,
the sun digs silver out of the evergreen.
Orchards of Syon, tenebrous thresholds
of illumination, a Latin love
elegist would comprehend your being
a feature of his everlasting dark.

I desire so not to deny desire's
intransigence. To you I stand
answerable. Correction: must once have stood.
What's this thing, like a clown's eyebrow-brush?
O my lady, it is the fool's confession,
weeping greasepaint, all paint and rhetoric.
Empower the muse; I'm tired. Shakespeare, who scarcely
brooded on perfection, perfect so many times.
Memory! memory! *The eye*
elaborates its tears, but misremembered,
misremembering no less key-clustered
mistletoe, the orchard's châtelaine.
I may well carry my three engraved thoughts
out beyond Shrawley whose broad verges once
throve like spare garden plots with pear and apple
or with wild damson, thinner on the ground.
O my lady, this is a fool's profession
and you may be dead, or with Alzheimer's,
or happily still adoring a different
Duke of Illyria. I have set you up,
I confess thát, so as not to stint
your voice of justice. Love grows in some
way closer to withdrawn theology.
The Deists' orb drops below Ankerdine.

Suicide-comedy, the panic-laughter
traversing, then cut off; and still a need
to be on the right side of this, survive
myself, garland myself with tribute.
How deeply wedded wére you? A strange
bisexuality of language
in private monodrama ís allowed
although disturbing. Did I disturb
in Klagenfurt or Rome, dead Ingeborg,
when ruins hooked and shelved the broken
cloud-breaking moon? Prophets as fantasists
fulfilled — that's not the issue. *Scotus shows
necessity reconciled with free will* — HOPKINS,
himself soul-strung, haggard, though not like you.
You leave me with a ghosted speech to finish
saying we never met. False evidence,
and I'm a stalker — incapacitated —
of my own gifts and yours. Such prurient
language of flowers Parnassian, a blight:
gothic monk's hood, black horehound, but no longer
luxuriantly or *in rare abundance*. Still
inconsolable, sex-haunted, we'll reverse-
charge our challenge to the bridal suite.
Some voice will pick it up before refusing.

Reading Dante in a mood of angry dislike
for my fellow sufferers and for myself
that I dislike them. Dante is exact
in these conferrals. The words of justice
move on his abacus or make a sudden
psst psst like farrier's hot iron on horn.
The small blue flame of the glass votive lamp
that jibs in the funnelled air at the right
hand of Mary Mediatrix is his also.
From this distance the many barbed divisions
between Purgatory and Hell appear blurred.
You could step across or shake hands. Logic
is fierce, though at the last less feral
than mock-logic that destroys many.
Sensuous is not sensual, but such knowledge
increases with sensuality — *psst psst* —
hissing and crying out, the final throes.
Messaline — FRÉNAUD — *la vulve*
insomnieuse — ever-working valve-part
unsightly, blood-gravid. Look, Virgin
of Czestochowa, shelterer
from the black rain, look, ser Brunetto
whom Dante loved, look, Farinata: the sun
moves a notch forward on the great wheel.

La vida es sueño, and about time;
about hanging in there, about my self,
my mind as it is, to be remembered,
regarding timegraphs: these I understand
as the nongrammatical speech of angels.
I mean, they're beyond grammar that reminds
us of our fall, and of hanging out there.
My mind, as I know it, I still discover
in this one-off temerity, arachnidous,
abseiling into a pit, the pit a void,
a black hole, a galaxy in denial.
Life ís a dream. I pitch
and check, balanced against hazard,
self-sustained, credulous; well on the way
to hit by accident a coup de grâce.
Intolerable stress on will and shall,
recovery of sprung rhythms, if not rhythm;
test of creation almost to destruction —
that's a good line; it can survive me.
In denial not my words. I'm moving
blindly, all feelers out. Cosmic flare-wind
tilts the earth's axis, then returns us,
with our ears singing, our eyes rolled back,
mute, Atlantean.

Never cared much for righteous WICLIF. His
heavenly country meant the Kingdom of Heaven.
Chosen by and for the elect. A man need not
conform to his own words though he enacts
or enables them. Orators marginalized
by their own oratory a recurrent theme,
commonplace the cartographics of dissent.
All along, I'm labouring to try out
a numen that endures, exactly placed:
some upper valley in the high fell country
where millstone grit juts against limestone; shippens
built of random masonry; the home-
croft with its gapped wall and its well,
and black nettles where the privy stood. Ivy
and other evergreens in profusion,
most notably when it's winter. Yet Hardy's
redoubtable friend asked: Our people,
where áre they? — cranky old BARNES — *But óh,*
our peóple, whére are théy? And I could
not answer, but left him there in silence.
Curlew and kestrel trek the fell-sides,
the Hodder burls, a pheasant
steps from its thorny hedgebank beside us,
the stooped pear-tree honours us with its shade.

Stuck on then plucked off: self-surmounting rôles,
each one a self-presumption. Not any more
a wrought Jesuit or young
refusnik ǀ with an óld heárt. These
congested subway cars! We can
always say no, every last one of us.
So much is surely consonant with even
a fool's kind of street-wisdom. The heart
itself made to pull gears. Not now Péguy's
disciples or the helotries of Maurras.
Vanished the threatening and so threatened Jew.
Not for this time a student of war
Clausewitzian, despoiler of Goldengrove
and Syon's Orchards ǀ ás I have heard
myself sáy with some reason. Neither a slave
nor the slave's master-mistress. Not her
in such bravery, not him who answers
with proud erectile tissue. Casuistries
for which our tongues' tongue is choric
wherewithal ǀ and uninsured third party.
The heart is not beautiful. Exposed
it leaps fattily, apes a sexual motion
as if copulating with itself, *la vulve
insomnieuse*, to re-transplant FRÉNAUD.

Black, pinko-grey, brown, red-brown, yellow, all
here acclaimed vast Progeny's prodigies
in gross *Family of Man* register. WHO
HE arrives, departs, turns one
way or another, sees little play, less give.
If singular in achievement, mis-
governs himself and others. Even so
heterogeneity renders us equal
in broadly irregular ways. Laugh, damn you!
Scar-aspirant-star Coriolanus,
not now astronomical. Herod, our
relict, ultimate bluffs called in, patron
of rank opportunists, let
him not be forgotten. Good to hear
the seven Hebrew-Latin Penitential Psalms,
after some lapse, claim for despair a status,
something I cannot do. More than a mood-
intensifier you múst grant, undistraught,
and with acknowledgement to self as agent;
retractions if called for; codicils
drawing off satire. Initiative — that
New Age *pomerium* between Salford
and Manchester: not só far the Orchards
of Syon grown to be ours.

Myth, politics, landscape; with language
seeding and binding them; marram grass or
MILTON's broadcast parable *springing up*
armed men. All wisdoms thrown, as clay is thrown
and thrown again by the novice-master.
Our patience proven in the rage of others:
Commonweal their lodestar, inordinate
dominion their enterprise.
Love justice in a word, the knot-garden
of equity. Melech-Melchizedek, great
king among smallholders. *Righteousness*,
word of a decent splendour. Fortuna
our wire-dancer, or gyroscope — better
not look down. Existence ís
advanced mechanics, intuitively structured.
Kierkegaard springs to mind and is gone
as swiftly into the prodigal rainbow.
I can see only so far; I can say
only so much; I trust I shall greet you,
with or without your recognition,
instantly, and at my own expense. To, from,
the body of self-being *kommt Freud und Leid*:
joy, sorrow, as equals. All of this speaks well
for the affinities between us ǀ meeting as strangers.

Not the root of discrimination. That
coúld have been said more clearly: *crimen*. I'm
myself close to the inarticulate. Commonplace
muddledom I grant, extraordinary
common goodness being its twin. I think
of others on such evenings, long forgotten,
placing new flowers in the cemetery;
a sycamore's disproportionate
summer heaviness, engorged with shadow,
yew-bark, its waning glow, fulvous as sandstone;
empurpled bronzings: highlighted,
the beech's massive casque. Such grace
dispeopled, do not ask too much of it,
heart's fulness troubled by its own repose.
But is thís asking too much, of nature
and of relationship, of kind? Yes,
to be blunt: eloquence moving
bad conscience forward, backward, across,
like a metal detector. Owenite
Pity was excellent when burdened. These
new drafts on old devotion: who knows what
bolt has them targeted, what final tour
of sick Compassion: Shock-Horror's century
so unbelievable it must be true.

This is my shoelace. That is bobbled clover.
Here's a youngish man embarks on *I*
am an old man now. Eximious 'STARRY' VERE,
lyric and futile. Sit here, Memory.
A trial playthrough: they could hardly tell
prelude from postlude, postlude from intermezzo.
You're right! Not clover; even more tenacious,
tight like plantar warts or splayed pseudopods
that gardeners gouge and burn from lawns. Let's think
around the nature of impasse: metaphysics'
biochemical mystery. Wisdom
conspires with unwisdom, in a phrase
the genius of the maker — slog-and-slang.
Fancy's not truth, even if truth's confined
to Imagination: STC's compunctions,
the last bit of *The Tempest*, ancient prayers
of intercession that are said to work.
Melville's predisposition stood at bay
to public humours. Through stiff metaphrase
the sad man breaking in his stupent heart,
his stupent heart hog-tied on Southport sands
for Hawthorne to excogitate. I'll name
my own late fancies *Dream Children* if not —
just for the shine on it — *Prospero's Farewell*.

Not quite heat- or rain-scrim, this heavy
blankness, thinning now, presides with a mauve-
tinted wipe-around grey. Noon, yet no distance
to any horizon. The Malverns gone in haze.
I would not, formerly,
have so described bereavement. *Land
of Unlikeness* a similitude, certitude
moves to dissolution. Still, an answer:
misprised, misplaced love,
our routine, is not tragedy;
misadventure at worst. And my self-styled
lament must cover for us both.
Something here to know time by, in all
conscience. In all conscience we
shall lie down together. Dear one, be told
you chose impenetrable absence; I became
commonplace fantasy's
life-sentenced ghost. Allow
our one tolerable *scena* its two minds.
Abruptly the sun's out, striking a new
cleave; skidding the ridge-grass, down steep hangers;
buddleia in dark bloom; a wayward covey
of cabbage-whites this instant [|] balanced
and prinking; the light itself aromatic.

Belated grief-dervish: moribund and only
now into the surge and swing of the elements.
And not my words alone, as I commit them
to you also, yoú being my last but one
love. This could as well be lichened rock
or shadows of stained glass, Rossetti-like,
glowing and fading; ebbing, you might say.
Thát tell you what love is, how it stands, how
it opens itself, mirrors itself blind;
how it is self-requiting, not disarmed;
who makes it, who falls hard by the way
like carnal Christians or lost picaros;
poorly attended, guarded, self-exposed,
self-perpetuating, selfless, barren;
poison ivy or shingles for hair-shirt?
Imagination under stress in due
time becomes carbon, which I will not waste.
Who needs retractions? I can torment myself
with simple gratitude, municipal
salvias in the restyled garden of rest
staring my thoughts back. Beleaguered, roughly
unhostile people, many voices raised;
Messiah and *Elijah* filling the slate-
roofed tabernacles of millstone grit.

Cassandre à vingt ans: so that was your
grand exposition of the contraries?
And, yes, I do stress as if parsing.
Here is what we make of ourselves: grammar
implicated in, interpreting, the Fall,
a truism since Donatus. Good for him:
Syon's orchards ⎸ puffballs reared on dust.
This is the next-to-last time, probably,
that I shall visit them. Heart of my mind,
such is indebtedness íf this is not
faith it stays the bulk of experience: God's
grammar, as the poets once construed it.
In aureate vernaculars
we are old things of note. *Cassandre*,
I do go on. How do you, *ma chère
à soixante-sept ans*? Hear me out
Pleiade-style, mortality set aside;
you, deathless in my imagination.
But, for the present, show me — shów mé —
in fictive shape some average complex man
as he goes under, as he rises up,
swimming well through shifting densities
that press upon him and are not fiction
as I tell it.

Consummations, brimming or broken, *a master*
of exact fantasy — MANN, T., of Kokoschka.
Illuminating, though no stage is lit
that I can see. Then, *the uncompromising*
self-sufficiency of old age — H. TIETZE,
also apropos Kokoschka. But I'm
a malaprop and a misplacer
even as I speak. So, let me think,
obliviousness spites us. Concentrate
in face of oblivion. *Ce n'est pas drôle*.
Maria Casarès you too remember.
Droll Ingmar cloned her waxed appearance,
dead funny staring. One could live well,
a trouper of the soul's margins, *d'accord*?
Was Orphée's Princess │ Camus' lover and might
you be mý lover, íf we could
recover in ourselves forfeited mileage?
Vallombrosa, and deep other shade
and shadow places, valleys of dwale-drunk sorrows;
Goldengrove, the shuttered
lantern of nature. Syon's orchards
festal, unchanging, through the change of seasons,
burgeoning in that dream which is called vision
and naming, and ís for the centuries.

Heavy, post-cloudburst, slow drops, earthing, make
dibble-holes under the crouched evergreens.
So far I'm with you, conglomerate roots
of words. I wish I could say more. Even
this much praise is hard going. *Physical
psyche*, LAWRENCE, also hard going.
Nonetheless it's here: sodden, glaucous
evanescence; ridged *impasto*. I sense
revelation strike obliquely in,
thwartways, to our need.
Pigeon-mobbed, on the play-patch, my own
public madman hurls at the laden air
his archive of bagged injustice. Let us
not follow him into the *Theatre
of Kings and Magistrates*. My polity —
polity! — acts convalescent
with time and matter, each particular seam
of common being; close-set
quotidian marvels, fresh-felled trunks of beech
split thin-clean like slate. I claim elective
affinities ás of the root, even.
Even if unenduring. Treat with care
these angry follies of the old monster.
Dig the — mostly uncouth — language of grace.

Right, one more time! *Pomerium* will not
pass muster as *orchard*. That place of last
reckoning, at the Berlin Wall,
more resembled it; or say Carthage
chemically defoliate, salt understood
here as a chemical. Or the French con-
nection, *cordon sanitaire*? Contingent
natures of all things save God. *Uncompromising
self-sufficiency* work for the cockroach.
Difficult to end joyful starting from here,
but I'll surprise us. Inurements
I allow, endurances I approve;
nothing of ours is irreducible
though passion of failed loves remains
in its own selving. So let us
presume to assume the hierarchies,
Goldengrove, even as these senses fall
and die in your yellow grass, your landscape
of deep disquiet, calm in its forms: the Orchards
of Syon, sway-backed with pear and apple,
the plum, in spring and autumn resplendent.
Syon! Syon! that which sustains us and is
not the politics of envy, nor *solidarność*,
a hard-won knowledge of what wears us down.

But now and in memory never so
wholly awaited, the breadth of this
autumnal land. In Goldengrove the full
trees trumpet their colours: earth-casualties
majestic; unreal as in life they build
riches of cadence, not yet decadence,
ruin's festival. This much is allowed
us, forever tangling with England
in her quiet ways of betrayal. Natural
mother, good but not enough. Again, bring
recollection forward, weeping with rage.
Debit the lot to our chequered country,
crediting even so her haunted music.
Loyal incoherence not official
but now and then inspired: when circling
Heathrow on hold we are entertained
by Windsor's scaled-down perfect replicas;
or as Sussex, dormant, rippling with shadows
of airflow, tilts, straightens under, and they
switch off the flight-chart.
So much for my conclusion, a small
remembrance, *nos fidelités sont*
des citadelles — PÉGUY. Our fealties taken
to be your places of refuge and defence.

Never an off season. Call for the voicer
of fair omen. The voice persists
in rising monotone. Talk obsession
to ecstasy. Switch off *My Word*. Lie
down in the space provided.
Pollen and basalt — Dame Rainbow, ancient
lover of water, immortal
for want of a better term; self-remnant
in each element of the same desire.
Not as she once was, metaphysical
and, like, wild. Weigh the importunate
nature of being ⏐ with a light
husk, the grasshopper's, tall
storyteller of the Hesperides
with hymns to divine Aphasia
(*for it is she*). Even so Goldengrove
might have been Silvertown, could be Golders Green;
you can't rule on that. *Finis* was the last
word to escape me. Period. Stop
trying to amuse with such gleeful sorrow.
Here are the Orchards of Syon, neither wisdom
nor illusion of wisdom, not
compensation, not recompense: the Orchards
of Syon whatever harvests we bring them.

About the Author

Geoffrey Hill was born in Bromsgrove, Worcestershire, in 1932. A graduate of Keble College, Oxford, he taught for many years at the University of Leeds, then lectured at Cambridge as a Fellow of Emmanuel College. He is the author of eight previous books of poetry and of *New and Collected Poems, 1952–1992*. His stage version of *Brand*, a dramatic poem by Ibsen, was commissioned by the National Theatre, London, and performed there in 1978. His critical writings have been published in two volumes, *The Lords of Limit* and *The Enemy's Country*, the latter based on his Clark Lectures delivered at Cambridge in 1986. Since 1988 he has lived in Massachusetts and taught at Boston University, where he is currently Professor of Literature and Religion and co-director of the Editorial Institute.

About the Type

The text of this book was set in DTL Fell, a digitalized version of an anonymous Dutch typeface cut in the seventeenth century. The original is one of the three sets of type purchased as a gift to the Oxford University printing office by John Fell (1625–1686), Bishop of Oxford from 1675 until his death. In his book *The Roman, Italic, and Black Letter Bequeathed to the University of Oxford by Dr. John Fell* (1950), Stanley Morison argues that the font is the work of the outstanding Amsterdam punchcutter Christoffel van Dijck (1601–1669), but this remains to be proved. The Fell types are the historical link between Dutch Old Styles, such as Janson, and English Old Styles, such as Caslon. They have inspired the work of succeeding generations of typographers, from the German Peter de Walpergen (whose own adaptation of the Fell Roman, cut for Oxford University in 1693, was among the first old-style fonts cast in England) to the twentieth-century American Bruce Rogers.

Designed & composed by Wesley B. Tanner / Passim Editions,
Ann Arbor, Michigan.

Printed & bound by Edwards Brothers,
Ann Arbor, Michigan.